Ami,

Thank You :

AGELESS YOU

When You find Your
Purpose... You'll
find Your Passion!

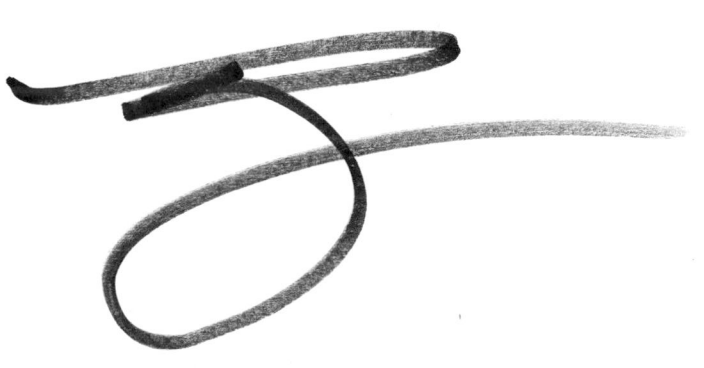

Thank You !

When you find Your purpose ... You'll find Your passion !

AGELESS
YOU

The Boomers Guide
To Beginning Again

TOM FABBRI

KEYNOTE PUBLISHING

Tom Fabbri
805 Main Street
Port Jefferson, NY 11777
tom@tomfabbri.com

ISBN: 978-0-578-10445-4

Contents

Dedication

I dedicate this book to my son Brandon... Every time I look at him I am amazed and filled with unbelievable love. My wish is that he lives his dreams as I live mine, and that he fills his life with *Passion, Purpose* and *Love*.

Acknowledgement

I would like to express my gratitude to everyone who has believed in me and encouraged me along this path that I have chosen. A path to live my dream life and change lives for the better along the way. I have my dark days for sure... but as a wise sage once said... Every passing moment is another chance to turn it all around. This book is written for you... now is the time to turn your life around.

Foreword

AS you are reading this book I feel safe to assume that you have either joined myself and Tom in the dreaded "middle years" of life or you're smarter than your average bear and are intent on getting here prepared, awake and stronger than most.

Either way, welcome. You have nothing more to fear.

It is true that this time can be an uneasy one for many—as by the time most people reach their 40's they are quietly suffering the ravages of [premature] aging. You are one of the fortunate ones. For, through whatever series of events, you are here, at this moment reading this book.

Tom's life, his bold adventuring spirit, is a shining example of the life you too deserve and are meant to enjoy. He's a man who has struggled and yet still strives, who has journeyed inward to the depths of his soul and propelled his body to the tallest points on Earth.

Too many "experts" and their followers waste time chasing extremes and overlooking the simple truth of what works. When you've pushed to the edges and beyond, when you've faced your fears, stared at death and embraced life, pure and simple truth is revealed.

That is what you will find in the practical life wisdom of Tom Fabbri and his guide to the Ageless You. Tom has simply, artfully and eloquently deconstructed the elements of a happy, healthy and successful life into 5 simple steps. You might think of these 5 as the essential building blocks for a long, vibrant and brilliant life.

Both Tom and I are here as living proof that this arching over and sliding down model is not a requirement. You can make a different choice— you can create a second ascent in life, regaining and reclaiming your strength, energy and vitality—and you can ride that higher wave into the rest of the best of your life.

If you're ready to be free from the oppression of a lifestyle and environment that is damaging your life and aging you long before your time; if you're not willing to let life "take its toll" accepting the default of a plummeting quality of life; this is your guide. Yes, you've come to the right place. Read this book and don't just do what it says, but be how it is—that means let it come in through your awakening mind, be here now, and live with that strength, awareness and clarity into the absolute best of your life.

Here's To Your Life and our World at Full Strength,

Shawn Phillips
Author, Strength for LIFE, ABSolution
Creator Full Strength Nutrition

Foreword—How the Good Life Is Killing Us

IT happened slowly, over the last fifty years I think. And in many ways, it was a good thing that "ease" and "comfort" became a cultural norm. The great depression was just that, depressing. The world war that followed included years of sacrifice and hardship and tragedy. Just getting through the day in those times preceding the 1950s required a real effort for most people.

Tom Fabbri – Author of *Ageless You*

It was a deserved thing that our way of life got better and continued to get better after that—even considering subsequent wars at home and abroad. America had earned a hard won break and our lives started to shift. We became more comfortable. Living, in many ways, simply got easier. And we began to expect it to be easier.

The 1,250 square-foot dream homes of our fathers, where they lived until they died, became starter homes for young couples on their way to 3,000 square foot mansions. Cars became cushier and began to come standard with a/c, of course. The average hotel room became luxurious. And work turned from something you did, often with your hands, to someplace you went. When you got there, you sat in a chair (a really nice one) for most of the day until you sooner rather than later, went home. Then, you and the family got back in the heated leather-seat car and went out to dinner. You came home and sat down on the couch and watched television on a screen that cost you half a month's salary (what your father spent on his first car), until you went to bed in a huge king-sized bed connected to a bathroom the size of the average kitchen in the 40's.

Yes, things have definitely gotten better. But in many ways *we* have gotten much worse. Study after peer-reviewed study clearly shows that we are less happy, less fulfilled, and less healthy than we once were. At the same time we are more stressed, more harried, and more overweight than generations before us. For all of the things that we have improved in our lives there seems to have been a cost—and it may have been us.

The way we have decided to live easier has made living altogether harder. It's harder on our bodies. It's harder on our minds, and harder on our overall happiness. Though modern medicine has us living longer (a little) we seem to be getting older sooner than we should. The way we live, the food we eat, the real work and effort we have designed out of our lives, have all conspired against us until we have become what Dr. Brene' Brown calls "the most in debt, obese, addicted, and medicated adult cohort in U.S. history."

You don't have to be that way. You don't have to get older before you've gotten truly old. You can un-change some of the ways that you now live so that you can truly enjoy the life you really deserve.

By making small slow changes in how you spend your time, how you eat and drink and move, and even in how you think, you can become a different version of yourself. You can become ageless--an ageless version of you. I know it is possible because I've done it. As I write this I am training to climb Mount McKinley, the fifth mountain on the fifth continent I have traveled to in reaching my goal to climb "The Seven Summits," the highest mountains on each continent. I'm 53 years old.

In this book, we will discuss the five areas of your life that you can change to become healthier, more active, and more alive than you may have been in years. Success is the progression towards a worthy ideal and together we'll formulate a plan for the changes you want to make with real strategies that will turn those ideas into realities. Included in this book are tools for redefining the your health and fitness goals, a discussion about the importance of your emotional well-being in living an effective and ageless life, and finally an exploration of healthy eating and exercise techniques that I've developed, techniques that are truly sustainable and effective for everyone. Finally, I'll make sure you know how to have fun, not just with the positive changes you will make for yourself, but with the rest of the fantastic life you will live.

Some things are so much better than they use to be. It's time for you to make everything better. It is time to live the life you deserve. I'm very happy to offer my new book, *Ageless You*—join me on an adventure into the truly and completely better life we have earned for ourselves.

~Tom Fabbri, 2011

From Passion To Purpose:

Creating a Plan You Can Live With

THERE is almost nothing so common as our dreams for a better life. Almost everyone thinks about his or her future as different or better than now. "I'll make more money, next year. I'll be thinner, next summer. I'll be happier, more fulfilled, and have more fun in my life.... tomorrow." Hope is universal. What isn't so common is hope fulfilled. Something seems to separate those who achieve their visions from those who only keep dreaming, or worse, lose that hope altogether.

That difference is purpose. Achievement of anything comes to those who take consistent and purposeful action to reach their goals. This is true of finances, and relationships. I. It's true of careers. And it is definitely true of health and fitness. Those who achieve their goals do more than just hope. They do something after they dream. They make plans and work their way into the future they envisioned.

By the end of this first chapter you will have defined your goals for agelessness and world-class health and laid the groundwork for the plan that will take you there.

Goal Setting and World Class Planning

Look at the difference in these two statements:

- I want to lose twenty pounds
- By July 15th, in order to be and feel healthier, I will lose twenty pounds through proper diet and consistent exercise.

They both say essentially the same thing—lose twenty pounds—but statement 2 is much more powerful. It has a deadline, it has a purpose, and it just seems so much more achievable. That's because statement 1 is raw hope. Statement 2 is a goal with a plan.

To help goals become reality, four things should happen:

1. Each goal should be made specific and given a deadline.
2. You must formulate a plan that makes sense.
3. You have to review the goal and its plan every day.
4. You have to remind yourself of the purpose and do the work.

These four steps turn hopes into reality.

Step 1—Making Goals Specific

The most critical step to achieving success in any area of your life is to envision it as if it has already happened. A clear picture of where you want to go is crucial to making it there. It's not enough to say, "I want to be in better shape." You need to have the added specifics that make the goal clear and achievable.

Of each goal you have, you want to get to these specifics:

- What and When and Why.
- A real goal answers the questions what, when, and why. A goal has a result, a timeline, and a purpose.

You can do it right now! Take out a blank sheet of paper and answer the following questions about your fitness.

What *Questions*

- **What would you like to look like?** Be specific. Write down waist size, amount of body fat, muscularity. Nothing is too detailed. Clothing goals are perfect for this question. "I want to fit into a size 6" or "into my 32 inch waist jeans." These are the specific, measurable things that real goals start with.
- **What do you want to weigh?** Is there a weight from your past you would like to reach again? Write it down. Have you been told by your doctor that you need to lose 30 lbs? Write it down.
- **What would you like to able to do?** This question is just as specific as weight. Would you like to be more flexible? Be stronger? This is a question about ability. Your answers might sound like. "I would like to able to run five miles with ease" or "I want to be full of energy, even into the late afternoon." Don't get wrapped up in what you think your limits are at this point. The how comes later—for now, just answer the questions as if you knew it could be done.

Did you write down your answers? If not, stop just for a minute and consider taking this first step and putting what you want down on paper.

When *Questions*

Now we need to define the **when** for these **what's**. It's been said that a goal is a dream with a deadline. Sure, that's a little cliché but there is a useful lesson for us in that one. You need to put a timeline on your goals. You're going to use these answers to gauge your progress, adjust your plan, and create new goals when the time comes.

If you actually did the **what** *work, that's awesome! So many people wait to take action. If you haven't done it yet, it's OK—go ahead and do it now.*

So next to each **what** answer (go back and do that work if you haven't) write down the answer about **when**.

For instance, you want to fit back into your size 32 jeans or your size 5 dress? Great! By when? Here is where a good honest look at your current fitness is necessary. We live in the age of the "quick fix" and the "miracle diet". Like I said in the beginning—the ageless lifestyle isn't about quick fixes and fad dieting: It's about reality.

How long did it take you to from those jeans you want to get back into to the ones you wear now? If it took ten years to get into the kind of shape you are now, nothing will get you back there in a month. You **can't** safely lose 20 lbs in 4 weeks. For deadline questions about weight, I suggest considering *not more than 2.5 lbs a week.*

For all the other questions, decide on when you want them to happen by (a specific date, month day and year) and write the dates down.

Why *Questions*

One last time now, go back to each goal and think about **why** you want those things. This is one time where negative answers can actually help you. "We will do far more to avoid pain than to gain pleasure." Anthony

Robbins has said (and proven). "Because I am sick of being fat!" is a great answer to why you want to lose weight. You can add the positive "and I'll feel much better" but having the negative will be a motivator as well. "Because I want to be alive for my granddaughter's wedding" is a great reason to quit smoking.....or drinking too much.

Let yourself go deep into all the reasons that you want the things you want. There are no wrong answers here either—be real with yourself. Get mad if you have to but write down, next to each goal, **why** you want the things you do.

Having answered the what, when, and why, you now have on a sheet of paper a clear set of specific fitness goals. You have taken your hopes and turned them into achievable ideas for your life with a timeline for that achievement.

Step 2—Formulate a Plan

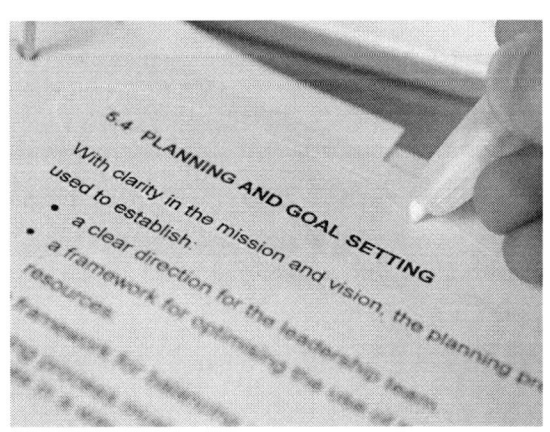

The point is not to agonize over a specific day-by-day blueprint. But you need to come up with some actionable things to get you started. And let's be clear: the plan you start with will not be the plan you finish with. You will adjust and change and learn from the actions you take. Working a plan is about the small steps you will take to get you to your larger goal.

You may start with a plan to do 30 minutes of cardio workout 6 days a week. You may eventually work up to 45 minutes or more a day. Perhaps you will need to work up to that level by staring with a plan to work out 15 minutes a day. As you start to work your plan you will get a better idea about its effectiveness. Your plan, like your goals, needs to be flexible—not to give yourself an "out" if you aren't reaching your goals, but to help you find ways to adjust your actions to help meet your goals.

Yes, your deadlines might need to shift. You may reach them sooner than you thought. Or perhaps you were too ambitious and need to change the plan. That's all fine. The important thing is to actually **have a plan** and work at it every day. The adjustments will come later.

As I stated before, success is the progression of a worthy ideal. **Your goals are the worthy ideal; the plan is a tool you will use to make the progression real.** Many of the questions you have about what to put into your plan and what to do first will be answered in the chapters that follow. When you come back to writing your initial plan you will be able to use the information about diet and exercise in this book to help formulate a plan.

Your plan is something that needs to be written down. You can use journals or your computer, as long as you can easily and readily access the plan daily.

Step 3—Looking at your Goals Every Day

Looking at your goals every day is an important part of changing your behavior, and it is a behavioral shift that needs to take place to meet the deadlines you've set. Meeting deadlines requires you to behave in a manner consistent with your goals. For that, you need to be reminded where you are heading every day. Otherwise it is too easy to drift off into old habits. Keeping your goals "in your face" makes it easier to act like you mean them.

If your goal is "I will lose 20 lbs in four weeks because the extra weight is affecting my heart," and you have that goal on your refrigerator and on your desk at work, it becomes very hard to eat pizza for lunch. If eating pizza for lunch (or an equivalent "bad" food) was your old habit, then seeing your goal in writing—along with the purpose for it—several times a day will help change you.

Seeing is believing...and physically seeing your deadline, goal, and reasons for the goal will make a believer out of you by influencing the decisions you make.

There are other things you can use to help you reach your goals that serve as constant and daily reminders and help you make good decisions. The numbers from your last cholesterol test, that picture you hate that makes you look fat, or one at the weight you want to reach again, these are all good visuals that will remind your purpose for making quality changes in your life.

So make copies of your goals. Read them every day. Put them in places that make it impossible not to see them. Adjust them as needed, cross them off when you reach them and set them again; but keep them in front of you. Keep them in on your mind so the next step of actually doing the work will be something you know you want to do.

Step 4—Doing the Work and Paying the Price

Paying the price.. Sounds dramatic, doesn't it? It isn't. If your dreams are big, and I hope they are, remember that the steps to get there don't have to be. With your goals in front of you and as constant and daily reminders, and following your plan, your visions will become realities by taking small manageable actions. There doesn't have to be a massive shift in your world.

You don't have to spend hours a day, every day in the gym (unless your goal is to become a world class bodybuilder or an Olympic athlete). You don't have to completely change everything you eat all at once and radically change your diet. Doing the work is about making the smart choices and working the plan you have made to reach your goals, every day. Paying the price is about making the small choices that will all add up and eventually bring you to the realization of those hopes that you turned into goals.

Paying the price means giving up things that move you farther from your goals. It may mean giving up a certain type of junk food for the sake of your health, or getting up an hour earlier to fit your workout into your already hectic day. It may mean giving up your favorite television show and using that time for an activity that moves you closer to your goals.

Whether the timeline you set for your goals is measured in months or years, your goals will only come to you if you actually take action. Every day you will need to behave in a manner consistent with your goals. People who are losing weight do not eat junk food, so if that's your goal, you won't eat junk food. If the restaurant has a drive through window, it isn't for you. People who have vitality and health and stamina do not smoke; therefore, you can't. Instead, you will have to make the decisions that move you ever closer to your goals and farther away from the life-style that led you to where you are now.

Where you are now is a product of all of the small decisions you made over the past years. I'm not telling you anything you don't already know, am I? If you are not in the shape you want to be in and if you don't have the health and looks that you want, you know how you got that way. You got there by making small, almost inconsequential decisions that led you right to where you are. And it is small, almost inconsequential decisions that will take you to where you want to be. Paying the price is simply about taking personal responsibility for living the life you want.

Instead of ordering the steak and potatoes, you're going to order the fish and vegetables. Instead of skipping the workout, you're going to make it. Instead of watching the news after dinner, you'll take a long walk. Instead of staying up late, you'll get a good night's sleep. You're going to start acting like the person you envisioned yourself to be. Soon, that acting won't be acting anymore. Those choices will become habits and those habits will become your lifestyle. Accomplish that and your goals will arrive without warning and your dream for a better life will become real.

The Importance of Unseen Things

The Mind—Body—Soul Connection

"Every action and feeling is preceded by a thought."

~ James Allen

WE rarely want things for what they are. Instead we want things for how we think they will make us feel. If you want more money, it isn't because you like dollar bills. It's because you equate more money with less pressure, more fun, and an easier life. The feeling that "real" diamonds convey makes them more desirable than the equally brilliant cut glass. We all want the things we can see because we desire the things we can't see.

The connection between what we want and why we want it is a positive and powerful thing. But it isn't enough just to brush by that truth and move on. We must pay attention to and nurture those things inside of us that make the outside world we want a reality.

If you want to be healthier, thinner, stronger, or anything else that can be seen, then you have to consider (often) what unseen things you are really looking for.

Our minds, bodies, and souls are not completely independent things. You cannot effectively change one without changing the others. So if you want to improve your body and live an ageless lifestyle, then you need to work on the unseen things in your life. You have to work on your mind; you have to nurture your spirit, and you have to connect those to your body in meaningful ways.

Reading

> "The man who doesn't read good books has no advantage over the man who can't read them."
>
> ~ Mark Twain

In our new shiny digital world it has become very easy to be a non-reader of what Twain called "good books." The web offers up a huge variety of things to read, but you have to be careful. Consider what you spend time reading, and almost as importantly, what you don't.

What you read is a diet to your mind just like food is to your body. Short reads like blog posts, magazine articles, and everything you ever read in the newspaper, are snacks. They are always compressed versions of much larger ideas. Some of them are good snacks, and some are bad, but they are not enough. If you don't spend significant time reading books, you are mal-nourishing your mind in the same way that snacking alone would malnourish your body.

Books (Twain's "good books") are deep and full explorations into broad ideas that truly inform your mind and intuition. They truly educate you in ways that articles and blog posts cannot. Most importantly, the taking in of those complete and fully developed ideas allows you to credibly share that knowledge with those around you, just like properly nourishing your body allows you to do useful physical work.

Quality Down Time

Besides the deep exploration of full ideas that you get from them, reading books provides real down-time that web-reading and television watching (especially news shows) can't. Sitting in your favorite chair, deeply engrossed in a good book with your thoughts, is deeply restorative. It is calming and just plain good for you.

How Much

In Tim Sanders book, *Love is the Killer App* (read it), he espouses the 80/20 rule for books over articles (web or otherwise). Eighty percent of what you read should be books. Sanders calls them "thought meals" compared to the articles that are "ideas-lite" or snacks. I agree. Most of what you read should be the full, well-balanced meals provided in truly good books.

Fact or Fiction

Your 80% shouldn't be made up of modern fiction alone. You can spend a year reading nothing but Stephen King or J.K. Rowling, but it won't do much for you other than to entertain your imagination. Fiction is fine, but you need balance in your book diet like everything else. Read books on health and nutrition, for example. Learn things about relationships and communications. An excellent biography of someone you admire or respect is always a good read and will help you to grow.

In the end you must grow your mind through reading and lifelong learning to really change the way you think and therefore how you act. If you take advantage of the benefits that reading provides, your physical transformation will be made an easier and more lasting thing.

Journaling

"If your life's worth living, it's worth recording."
~ Anthony Robbins

The next best practice to nurture the mind is to journal. Writing in a journal daily actually liberates the mind by giving the things you think about, worry about, dream about, and just mull over in your head every day a place to sit. The act of writing it down allows you to let go of it long enough to work through those worries and fears and thoughts and actually do something about them.

It's the same thing that happens when you make a list of any kind. For example, writing a simple grocery list allows you to literally forget about what you need and carry those thoughts in your pocket. Imagine trying to carry that list of items in your head from your kitchen to the store. You always forget something that way. Journaling does to thoughts what lists do for the things you need: it allows you to let them go and to use your mind for the other things.

You should also write what you are grateful for. I have found this to be a great stress reliever, personally. By taking all of my thoughts and writing about them in my journal every morning I reaffirm what I am grateful for in my life and what I need to work on to make things better. By writing about my goals and how I am progressing towards them, they are made more real for me and present in my mind throughout the day.

You can do this electronically, but I prefer a really good notebook. By using something solid and well made, leather covered with quality pages, it becomes a daily ritual and feels more permanent. When I start to feel that I'm not doing enough, or that my own progress is too slow, it helps to look back a few months (or years) and remind myself of how far I have come. Journaling makes that possible in a way your memory cannot.

Say Nice Things

Another great practice is to say affirmations, or mantras. So many of us have spent years playing tapes over and over in our heads that have talked us out of so much. Do you recognize any of these gems?

"I'll never have a home like that one."

"She would never want to be with a guy like me."

"I'll never look like her. I'm too heavy."

"Wow, it must be nice to….."

These things we say both out loud and in our thoughts have a profoundly negative effect on us. Whether we say them often or not, they are heard by our minds and effect our spirits and always in a bad way.

Affirmations—yes, I mean saying things out loud to yourself—are helpful to undo the negativity that those old phrases of lack and longing have wrought in our lives so far. You need to hear the words spoken, out loud and into your ears so they can change how you feel. They change how you feel about yourself and how you feel about yourself determines the actions you take.

An affirmation that I use on a daily basis is
"I am strong, calm and confident." By repeating this
over and over, saying it throughout the day, the words
become thoughts and I feel strong, calm and confident.

One friend of mine who was struggling with learning a massive amount of information for his job started saying to himself, "I remember things easily and well. I remember everything I read." That daily mantra became a reality for him and completely changed his career. In his youth he was a terrible student and always told himself he wasn't that smart. By changing how he talked to himself he became an expert in his field by becoming a voracious reader who "remembers everything he reads easily and well."

How have your thoughts and words worked to hold you back? What negative tapes have been playing over and over in your head? If you have been saying things like "It is so hard for me to lose weight," or "I don't like going to the gym," then change the way you talk to yourself by actually, you know, talking to yourself. Say things like "I am reaching my goals by eating healthy and I feel so much better now." If you don't enjoy exercise, that's OK—but shut up about it! Say instead "I love the feeling of accomplishment after I finish a workout."

Say the things you want for your life, out loud and often, and they will become easier to act on and make them real.

Release from Fear

Fear is the single most destructive force in our human psyche when it's not used to our advantage. Most people let fear rule their lives. They are afraid of poverty, ill health, criticism, death, and the loss of love. Fear makes us want to take action, always, and when fear is unfounded, any action we take to ward off the danger can create unwanted consequences.

For example, fear of rejection makes us keep people at length so they can't reject us, right?

In its useful state, fear creates energy that is designed to increase performance and help us play at a higher level. Our bodies actually create adrenaline when we become scared or fearful. It's how we use this adrenaline that counts the most. Understanding and using fear constructively is the tricky part. Feeling the fear and harnessing its power will actually empower you to do better.

In her bestselling book, *Feel the Fear and Do It Anyway* Susan Jeffers says that fear will always be a part of our lives in one form or another. And this applies to everyone. She says that no matter who we are, where we live and what we are experiencing in life, we all feel fear, but fear doesn't need to hold us back from living a rich and beautiful life.

Fear of anything keeps you from doing it—even though we might otherwise be great at the very thing we fear (think public speaking or great singers with stage fright).

She is right—isn't she? From my experience I have found that if you respect fear and face it head on and act, what you'll find is not terror but an excitement that will bring you moments you will never forget.

One way to confront the things you are afraid of and take action anyway is to think them through to their worst possible outcome. Literally ask yourself what is the worst possible thing that can happen with this thing that I am afraid of? Often you come to the conclusion that it isn't so bad after all, and the risk is worth the gain.

One man came to this conclusion when analyzing his fear of public speaking. He determined that the worst thing that could happen would be that he would bomb onstage, they would think he was a terrible speaker, and never ask him to speak again. So he was actually turning down speaking requests for fear of not getting speaking requests. Think about your own fears in that way and they often turn out to be just as irrational.

Your Body Takes Notes

One of the most important factors in your overall health is how your mind can control your physical well-being. Studies have shown most convincingly that the fear of disease, even where there is not the slightest evidence of actual illness, often produces the physical symptoms of the disease feared.

In one analysis of 19 clinical trials of antidepressants, when comparing placebo control group results to actual users of the drugs, the "expectation of the cure accounted for 75% of the drug's effectiveness, not related to chemical changes occurring in the brain." The two ideas that "I think I am sick therefore I am," and "A drug is effective because we believe it is" can be instructive for us in our daily lives.

Dr. Paul Ekman, an expert on facial expressions and author of numerous books on emotions discovered that not only do our emotions play out on our faces, but that if we mimic the expressions of emotion, we actually begin to feel physiological change because we made the faces. If you look up and smile, you become happier. If you make an angry facial expression, then you will begin to physically feel anger. The emotion and the outward evidence of the emotion are linked. In the same way, stress and anxiety (emotions that accompany real illness) have been linked to a higher incidence of illness.

This is why is it so important to take care of your mind and emotional states as well. Stress and tension are real killers to your health. Happiness, being calm, and real relaxation are truly good medicine. Your body listens to your mind for cues on how to feel. Tell it good things.

Discovering Your Soul

All of this that we have discussed and will continue to discuss in this book, from your goals and aspirations to the way you talk to yourself and take care of your body, are all parts of the discovery of who you truly are. All of this is about the outward manifestation of your authentic self. Like Michelangelo, who spoke of chipping away at the marble to remove everything that wasn't the figure inside, so you have to work on chipping away all of the things that aren't you.

The goals you set were about becoming what you want for yourself and how you see your own potential. They represent the you that is possible. To get to that person, you need to become that person emotionally as well. Your mind and spirit must match up with that better you first.

So spend real time relaxing through meditation and reading. Write down your thoughts and dreams for the better life you envision. Talk to yourself and others about the real and positive things you envision for your life. These unseen things are a real part of who you are and their development shouldn't be left to circumstance. They deserve as much of deliberate action as anything you will ever do in the gym. How you nurture these unseen things is just as important as how you nurture your body. Your mind, body, and soul are connected and changing one means changing the others.

Living the ageless lifestyle isn't just something to be done in the kitchen and through exercise. Though the next chapters are all about those things, they are certainly not everything. Remember while on this journey for a newer more youthful you, that you don't want to just look a certain way. You want to be the totally authentic and complete person you've always known you should be, inside and out.

Eating on Purpose: Feeding Your Body

A Diet for an Ageless Body

OF all the decisions we make in our lives, rarely is anything as impor-tant as what we choose to eat and drink.

When you first read a statement like that it seems like an overstatement, I know. But I'm not talking about what you ate last night in particular. It's not about one meal or another, but rather what you choose to eat and drink consistently most of the time. Those decisions have a greater impact on your health and overall well-being than any others.

There are literally hundreds of exercise models out there: yoga, free-weights, step-aerobics, spin, Pilates, Tai Chi, running, etc. But which one of those you do is not nearly as important as the deci-sion to work out in the first place. There isn't an exercise program that makes things worse for you. But that isn't true of food. The foods you eat matter a great deal. How you feed your body consistently will determine at least 80% of your success in achieving your health and fitness goals.

You've always known this. No adult has ever eaten a donut and thought, "This is exactly the kind of thing that will keep me slim." You know that what you eat matters….a lot. But to reach your goals you are going to have to start consistently acting like you know it.

Small Steps

If you developed eating habits that are say…less than great…and the following nutritional advice represents a drastic change, then just like every other change it will take time and patience to create. Drastic changes in diet rarely last. You can't go to the gym and exercise on the first day as if you'd been going for a year already. It takes time to adjust. Believe it or not, you will need to allow your body to adjust to new habits and new foods as well.

Listen to your body!

This is one of the most important principles in this series of recommendations. If any food or supplement makes you sick in any way, stop it immediately. Trust your body to provide you better indications of what is good for you. When you follow this lifestyle plan you will notice a remarkable improvement in the way that you feel within a few days to a week; but if anything makes you feel worse, remove it from your plan.

For those of you I just lost because you "love" bread or you can't live without French fries – don't despair just yet. There are some very good alternatives to those things you love so much and I promise, you will find new things to love as you slowly change the way you eat.

1st Step, Avoid the Following Foods

The following foods are all highly allergenic and will frequently keep your immune system in overdrive by continually triggering the inflammatory response:

- Wheat (processed whole wheat products)
- White flour products such as cookies, pastries, baked goods
- Pasteurized cow's milk products

- Highly processed grain-based products **like the ones below** are not recommended.

  - Breads
  - Pasta
  - Cereal
  - Bagels
  - French fries
  - Chips
  - Pretzels
  - Waffles
  - Pancakes
  - Baked goods

2nd Step, Eat Live Foods

At least 1/3 of your food should be uncooked. Valuable and sensitive micronutrients are damaged when you heat foods. Cooking and processing food can destroy these micronutrients by altering their shape and chemical composition.

Many people eat plenty of calories and still suffer from malnutrition—nutrient deficiencies—from consuming a highly processed diet. It is one reason why many people cannot lose weight, because it leads to over-eating. If you're consistently feeling hungry, you're likely not getting sufficient amounts of the nutrients your body needs to thrive.

By simply adding live foods to your diet, you will feel (and be) more nourished and be less likely to over-eat to compensate.

Recommended Vegetables

Alfalfa	Escarole
Artichokes	Fennel
Asparagus	Garlic
Beet greens	Ginger
Beets	Green and red cabbage
Bok Choy	Kale
Broccoli	Kidney Beans
Brussel sprouts	Kohlrabi
Carrots	Lettuce: romaine, red leaf, green leaf
Cauliflower	Mustard greens
Celery	Okra
Chard	Onions
Chicory	Parsley
Chinese cabbage	Peppers: red, green, yellow and hot
Chives	Tomatoes
Collard greens	Turnips
Cucumbers	Spinach
Dandelion greens	Sweet Potato
Endive	Zucchini

3rd Step, Eliminate Sugar from Your Diet

Eating refined sugar weakens your immune system and promotes obesity, both of which are contributing factors to cancer. Every time you think about sugar, every time you even read the word on an ingredient label, you should replace it with "cancer fuel" because that's what it is: refined sugar = cancer fuel.

A weak immune system in and of itself is guaranteed to impair your health and promote virtually every disease known to man.

High sugar consumption can also lead to adrenal exhaustion, common symptoms of which include feeling mentally and emotionally stressed, sugar and salt cravings, moodiness, and feeling weak and lethargic.

Avoid most natural sweeteners (including corn syrup, high fructose corn syrup, fructose, honey, sucrose, maltodextrin, dextrose, molasses, rice milk, white grape juice, sweetened fruit juice, brown rice syrup, maple syrup, date sugar, cane sugar, corn sugar, beet sugar, sucanat and lactose).

All non-diet sodas have 8 teaspoons of sugar in each can. Most packaged cereals have sugar as their major ingredient. Diet soda isn't a healthy choice because of the toxic effects of artificial sweeteners, and the sugar from regular sodas is a completely avoidable peril.

Note: Eliminating sugar is going to be tough. It is everywhere and American adults eat about 22 spoonfuls a day. You are going to have to pay attention to labels (tip: the best foods don't have labels) and simply quit purchasing those items where sugar is high on the list of ingredients.

Artificial sweeteners should be avoided at all costs; they are simply toxic, all of them. The research isn't complete and the verdict isn't in, but everything I have read states they could have devastating effects. A very good resource for more on the subject is *Sweet Deception* by Dr. Joseph Mercola.

4th Step, Plan a Menu (or Eat on Purpose)

Not planning to eat is a huge contributor to poor diet choice. If you don't plan ahead for lunch, then ducking into the nearest restaurant is the easiest thing to do. If you don't think about what you will eat for dinner and make sure everything is ready, then ordering out is more likely to happen.

Most people have great difficulty implementing real nutritional change unless they sit down once a week (at a time when you are well rested, fresh and relaxed) and plan every meal for the week ahead.

Yes, I just suggested that you take a half hour to an hour out of your busy life and devote it to deciding what you are going to eat every week. I promise that doing so will not only make you healthier with more energy, but it will become one of your favorite things to do.

A great practice is to prepare your meals ahead of time. For example, make your lunch for the next day before you go to bed. Decide what you will be eating for dinner before you leave the house in the morning. This allows you to go to the store if necessary, or take the appropriate items out of the freezer. The end of a tough day at work is not the time to test your will power. But if your dinner is planned and ready to go, then the decision has been made and you will eat in a manner consistent with your goals.

The 'Right' 10 Healthy Recipes

Believe it or not this is all that I use, and typically that is all the American family uses. Ten basic recipes is the average for what most of us have routinely worked into our lives. All we need to do is make sure that they are the "right" ten recipes and we'll move towards out health goals almost automatically.

I am all for variety, but all of us function better and properly when we consistently eat the same healthy food items. We all need lean proteins, quality carbs, and essential fats. I have found out through trial and error what works best for my body and how my body feels and functions on these food items. You are going to have to try different healthy foods until you find the ones that work best for you.

Protein

Proteins are nutrients that are essential to the building, maintenance, and repair of your body tissues. They are also the major components of your immune system and hormones. Most people don't eat enough protein. A person's required protein intake varies and depends on your sex, height, weight and exercise levels. Normal protein intake ranges from 20 to 50 grams at each meal.

Acceptable Proteins

Organic eggs, grass fed beef, venison and lamb. Chicken and turkey are acceptable if raised organic and cage free. Fish is also an excellent source of protein, because it contains all the essential amino acids required for the body to grow and maintain lean muscle tissue. Amino acids are the building blocks that make up protein. There are nine essential amino acids that the body cannot synthesize that must be taken in through protein (food). Vegetable protein is also acceptable, but should be combined with these other sources of lean proteins because vegetables do not contain any of the nine essential amino acids. Vegetable proteins include plants such as soybeans, spinach, green leaf lettuce, fruits and vegetables.

Carbohydrates

Carbohydrates provide fuel for your body in the form of glucose or (good) sugar. (Remember—NO refined sugar.)

There are two types of carbohydrates—simple and complex. Simple carbohydrates are sugars, such as the ones found in candy, fruits and baked goods. The simple sugar in fruit is the acceptable simple sugar; the candy and baked goods contain the refined sugar we have to avoid.

Complex carbohydrates are starches found in beans, nuts, vegetables, and whole grains. While both grains and vegetables are carbohydrates, most (not all) grains should be avoided and most vegetables are acceptable. Your body prefers the carbohydrates in vegetables rather than grains because it slows the conversion to simple sugars like glucose, and decreases your insulin level. Grain carbohydrates, on the other hand, will increase your insulin levels and interfere with your ability to burn fat.

Acceptable Carbohydrates

Brown rice, steal cut oats, rolled oats, quinoa, yams, sweet potatoes, and Ezekiel bread are acceptable sources of carbohydrates.

Fats

Learning about fats can be confusing. When you go to the grocery store, you're confronted with advertisements telling you that a product is low in fat, or a product is made with partially hydrogenated oil.

To make sense of all the labels, I've compiled the following list of definitions for you:

- **Saturated fats:** These are found in animal products such as butter, cheese, whole milk, ice cream, cream and fatty meats. They are also found in some tropical plants and vegetable oils such as coconut, palm and palm kernel. Saturated fats are not as dangerous as you think. In fact, coconut oil is quite healthy and is the oil I use for cooking since it is far less likely to be damaged through heating.

  A persistent fallacy is that saturated fat will increase your risk of heart attacks. This is simply another one of those myths that has been harming your health for the last 30 or 40 years. The truth is, saturated fats from animal and vegetable sources provide a concentrated source of energy in your diet, and they provide the building blocks for cell membranes and a variety of hormones and hormone like substances. When you eat saturated fats as part of your meal, they slow down absorption so that you can go longer without feeling hungry. In addition, they act as carriers for important fat-soluble vitamins A, D, E and K. Dietary fats are also needed for the conversion of carotene to vitamin A, for mineral absorption, and for a host of other biological processes.

- **Trans Fats,** These fats form when vegetable oil hardens, a process called hydrogenation, and can raise LDL (bad cholesterol) levels, and lower HDL (good cholesterol) levels, which of course is the complete **opposite** of what you need in order to maintain good heart health. In fact, trans fats—as opposed to saturated fats—have been linked to heart disease, clogging of the arteries, type 2 diabetes and other serious health problems.

- **Monounsaturated fats:** Virgin Olive oil is the best. Adults who consumed 25 milliliters (mL) or nearly 2 tablespoons of virgin olive oil daily for one week showed less oxidation of LDL ("bad") cholesterol and higher levels of antioxidant compounds, particularly phenols, in the blood. Antioxidants can help prevent oxidative damage, which is caused by free radicals, byproducts of the body's normal processes that can damage body tissues.

   The Mediterranean diet, which is rich in olive oil, fruits, vegetables and grains helps explain lower rates of heart disease in countries such as Italy and Spain, where people consume more than one third of their daily calories from fats high in monounsaturated fatty acids. These fats may help to lower total cholesterol and LDL cholesterol.

What to Drink

By far the most important element of your diet is **water.**

Water makes up more than 70 percent of your body's tissues and plays a role in nearly every body function, from regulating temperature and cushioning joints to bringing oxygen to your cells and removing waste from your body.

Drinking enough water is one of the most simple, basic, and important health steps you can take. If you drink the required amount of water to maintain a light yellow coloring of your urine you can easily avoid dehydration, which can have profound effects on your health. And you can be dehydrated (or less than optimally hydrated) and not feel thirsty.

Dehydration can also cause fatigue, dry skin, headaches and constipation.

Avoid ALL soft Drinks: Soft drinks have no redeeming value whatsoever. Both regular and diet sodas are potent contributors to a number of health challenges. For example, did you know that for every can of soda you drink per day, your risk of obesity increases by 60 percent? This is one of the easiest changes you can make to significantly improve your health. As far as **fruit juices** are concerned, I personally don't drink them, as they contain high amounts of sugar. That doesn't mean fresh squeezed orange juice is bad, but it is easy to lose track of just how many calories you are taking in when drinking fruit juice.

Beer, wine, and distilled spirits are OK in moderation. Moderate alcohol intake is defined as a 5-ounce glass of wine, a 12-ounce beer or 1 ounce of hard liquor with a meal. Coffee and tea are allowed, just avoid adding cream and sugar to these drinks and don't count them as your water intake.

A Few Words on Supplements

I believe you can obtain most of the nutrition you need from wholesome food. There are some exceptions, but it is quite rare that someone would really benefit from a shopping bag full of supplements, especially the synthetic varieties. Supplements are just that—something to supplement the nutrition you are not receiving through whole foods.

My Supplement Recommendations for an Ageless You

Maintaining a healthy digestive system and following sound dietary principles are the best ways, I've found, to promote optimal health. The reason for this is because 80 percent of your immune system is located in your digestive system, and a robust, well-functioning immune system is your number one defense system against all disease. Take the following two steps to help insure a healthy digestive system

Step one: Every morning for 7 days drink an 8-ounce glass of **ginger mint tea with lemon** and stir in 1 tablespoon of organic **psyllium husk.** The combination of ginger, mint, lemon and psyllium are a powerful source for intestinal health and colon care.

Step two: Add ground organic **flaxseed** to your oatmeal every day. Flax promotes regularity, supports normal functioning of the digestive tract and has a positive effect on cholesterol.

Vitamin D

Optimizing your vitamin D levels can help you to prevent as many as 16 different types of cancer as well as reduce your risk of numerous illnesses including:

- Heart disease
- Diabetes
- Rheumatoid arthritis
- Obesity
- Cold & flu
- High blood pressure

Vitamin D is found in foods like milk, eggs, fish and fortified orange juice. However, you only get an average of 250 to 300 international units (IU) of vitamin D per day from dietary factors alone, which is rarely enough to maintain optimal levels.

Fortunately, vitamin D is also made in your body after exposure to ultraviolet rays from the sun, and this is the ideal way to get vitamin D.

Aspirin

Taking 2 baby low dose aspirin a day can decrease the risk of getting colon cancer, esophageal cancer, prostate cancer, ovarian cancer and breast cancer-all by 40 percent. Aspirin does this through the reduction of inflammation throughout the body.

Food Summary

I've been researching nutrition, diets, food, and supplementation for most of my adult life. It would be impossible to fit comprehensive nutritional advice into a single chapter, but the basic tenants of planning and the choices described above can be an excellent first step in working towards your ageless health and fitness goals.

---

*Start with these first steps and we can work through what comes next together. Join me at **www.TomFabbri.com** where I post all of my favorite recipes and advice about nutrition and the ageless lifestyle.*

Move to Live

The Full Advantage Workout

WE humans are in a very strange time in our evolutionary history. In the last 50 to 100 years, roughly .00005% of our time here as a species, something incredible and unprecedented happened. We stopped moving. Personally, I think it started with the wheel, or maybe it was that pesky industrial revolution and Mr. Ford's assembly line; but whatever started it, we have ended up here in 2011 and we have taken the need to move out of the living equation. It simply isn't necessary anymore.

Just a few hundred years ago, living on the earth meant moving on the earth. The primary mode of transportation was walking (or running). To most people, a job meant lifting something or carrying something, or building... something...heavy...that needed to be lifted or carried.

There was a small group of those with wealth or power of some kind and who got carted around and didn't have to work too hard, but everyone else had to do things, physical things. A few hundred years before now, those things were harder and living meant walking farther and pulling and lifting and pushing heavier things around. Go back far enough and you'll find about a 100,000 year static period in our evolution were the human body was in almost constant motion. Moving was an essential part of staying alive. If early humans sat still for half as long as we do in a given day, they would quite simply be dead. The human body was designed to move.

Today, to go to shopping we walk 15 yards from the cushioned seat in our climate controlled home, brave the elements for 30 seconds until we sit down on another cushioned seat in our climate controlled cars, then search for the closest available spot in the parking lot. I mean, who wants to take ten more steps if you don't have to? Unlike just a few hundred years ago when only a small percentage of people lived in luxury, and everyone else had to do something physical, today only a small percentage do truly physical work (think lumberjack, construction worker, moving and storage crews) and everyone else, mostly, sits down to live. The very meaning of a job has changed from a physical thing, to something we do with our brains, usually from a chair. We have, for better or worse, and in a very short span of time designed movement out of our lives.

So what?

The problem is that we haven't designed our bodies out of our lives. We still have them and they were still designed to move. And all we're using them as is a good place to hang clothes. For the most part, we use them like Sir Ken Robinson joked, "as a way to get our heads to meetings." With the exception of the common pet (your dog is the only one in the house that can do nothing at all and people think it's cute) no other animal on earth uses their bodies less than we do. That is bad for them, because unlike all other machines that we own, your body is the only mechanism that gets better when you use it, and worse when you don't.

A body that moves often feels better, works better, gets sick less often, thinks better, is less susceptible to injury, and looks better. A body that moves often experiences the world in a totally different way too. Sleep is more restful and rejuvenating, thoughts are clearer and more focused, and sex is better for a body that moves and moves often.

A very close second to the fuel that feeds it, how your body moves is the next most important part of how well we live and thrive.

So what do we do?

We have to design movement back into our lives and we have to do it in a way that recognizes and appreciates the world we have designed for ourselves. We can't all quit our day jobs and chop wood for a living. Hopefully, the work you do brings value to someone and fulfillment to your soul and you should keep doing it. But we can also design some time in our day to move our bodies in way that respects their need to be moved, while at the same time meeting our need to get on with our lives: our families, our work, our interests. We can't move all day, but we can move in such a way when we exercise that we take full advantage of the time we have and the movements we make. One way to do that is my Full Advantage Workout.

The Full Advantage Workout

The Full Advantage Workout is a method for training and exercising I've developed that I believe is the most sustainable exercise methodology to create an ageless body. Put simply it is this:

The Full Advantage Workout is way of moving your body through an exercise routine that takes full advantage of each minute used and each motion made.

If you're going to exercise, and you must use that time as effectively as possible. There can be a huge difference between showing up to work out, and actually doing something of value while working out. Health clubs and gyms are full of people whose intentions are good, but achieve very little results. While I respect the fact that they show up at all, and any motion is better than no motion, I see so many people who spend

---

hours in the gym getting minutes of results. I want you to spend minutes in the gym (or your home) getting hours of results.

I am not talking about anything easy. Like reaching any worthwhile goal, creating an ageless body won't be easy, but it can be a lot easier than you think if you persistently…

- Show up to your own workouts
- Take full advantage of the time when you workout
- Take full advantage of your movements when you work out.

Showing Up

You should treat your appointments with the gym, or your home, or wherever you chose to exercise, as the most important and unbreakable meetings of the day. They are actually, very important. Your health is what makes everything else in your life possible and being faithful to your fitness goals is being faithful to everything and everyone else in your life. Making the time to exercise is putting the oxygen mask on yourself before helping the others around you. It is simply irresponsible to treat other things as more important than your health and fitness.

Imagine if you cancelled other things the way some people cancel their workouts when they feel other things are more important. You don't hear people say, "You know, I couldn't shower this week. I've just been so busy," or "Brush my teeth? Who has that kind of time?"

If you're serious about changing your life and living a healthful and vibrant life now, and you are if you've read this far, you must show up to your own workout and do the work.

Full Advantage of the Time

In the last seven years (age 46 to 52) I've won or placed in nine natural bodybuilding and fitness competitions. In the last two years I have climbed four of the Seven Summits—the highest mountains on each continent. I have never spent "hours a day" working out or exercising. As I write this, I am in the middle of my ninety-day training routine in preparation for climbing Mount McKinley. Deep in the middle of the most arduous training I do, I'll do two 45 minute sessions in the gym today. When I am not training for a competition, my workouts are one session of 45 minutes, with a rest day every sixth day.

Working out and exercising does not have to take very long. You do not have to take hours, or even a full hour, out of your day to be in fantastic shape. You simply have to take advantage of the time you have set aside to exercise and do just that: exercise.

Take a look around the average gym. Time is being wasted in a lot of ways. People stand around "talking" about working out or socializing. Other people seem to move through their routines but with little purpose or effort, and with lots of break time between exercises. The average person's hour-long workout can look like the average hour of professional football. In 60 minutes of game time the ball is in motion for less than six minutes.

When you exercise you should be doing something to achieve your fitness goal every minute that you are there. You have purposefully set that time aside to move, so for goodness sake, do it. Move. My workout routine consists of one event followed by another and another until the time is gone. Done properly, a weight routine is a fully aerobic workout as well. You should go from warm-up and stretching, then onto your exercises, not rushing or moving fast, but purposefully moving through the routine.

There should be a tempo to your time in the gym and to each set of exercises and to each rep. One thing is certain, if you have time to talk and that talking is coming easy, then you're doing it wrong.

Full Advantage of the Motion

If you've looked around the gym for time being wasted, then you have also seen motion being wasted. We have all noticed the "grunters" in the gym. Usually clad in tank tops or tight fitting Tees. They load up plate after plate of weight and push or pull it through a range of motion in one direction, relax and let gravity do its thing, then repeat. They swing their bodies to create inertia or lean back and arch to create some angle to make the curl easier or the too heavy squat possible. They are cheating.

Injury aside (and that's a big aside), at least these people are at the gym, which is better than being on the couch, but they waste a lot of effort and motion by failing to pay strict attention to the following three truths. When moving through your routines understand and believe the following (for a start):

- **Form matters more than anything:** The difference between doing an exercise and doing it with perfect form is huge. Form when working out isn't just important; form is foundational. If you get the form wrong, then everything else you do, weights, reps, resistance etc., will simply be more of the wrong thing. The price to pay for improper form is injury and, of course, a less effective use of your time and effort.

- **The amount of weight lifted matters *less* than anything:** Perhaps the silliest and most meaningless question ever used to gauge a person's fitness is "How much can you bench?" Unless it is your goal to win a bench press contest, the numbers on the weights are meaningless. Last year I won the Muscle Mania Universe competition. How much weight did I train with? I can't tell you. I simply don't remember. What I can tell you is that I used the right amount to keep proper form throughout the exercise, and that it was a lot lighter than you might be thinking right now. The number on the weights, like your age, is meaningless.

- **Use everything you have *every time*:** When you exercise your biceps, your legs should be working. When doing leg presses, your shoulders and arms should be flexing. Your abdominals and core muscles should always be flexed and tight. It requires total focus of your attention on every muscle you have. (If you were wondering where the hard part was, this is it.) With every exercise you do, fully activate every muscle you have. Remember, you are making maximum use of every motion during your workout. You should lower the weight with the same focused intensity that you use to raise the weight. Turn each exercise into a full body experience that uses every inch of every movement to work the muscles in motion and even the ones that aren't moving.

That last one—**use everything you have every time**—is the fundamental difference between the workout I do and the workout done by most. By engaging your entire body in every exercise, you can maximize the effectiveness of your workouts, using very little weight (if any), while lowering the risk of injury that can take you off your routine. In fact, in all my years of training, I have never been injured during a workout.

This kind of focused and full body engagement will take time to get right. Instead of just pushing the weights though space, you are going to find yourself intensely concentrating on every move you make. Your pace may be very slow at first as your body gets used to the idea of flexing your forearms to exercise your legs, and tightening your abs to work your shoulders. If you have never flexed every muscle in your body, it can be an intense experience. (Tip: Remember to breath—most beginners hold their breath during an exercise.) But with experience and consistency, your motions will feel more natural and you will find a rhythm to your training over time.

With proper form, the right (small) weights, and by using your full body when you exercise, you can dramatically change your body and your life.

What now?

You may have noticed that I just told you how to do something, without telling you what exactly to do. That's because I don't know. I would have to know what your goals are, what your body type is, what the answers are to such questions as how much weight you need to lose

---

and how you want to look.. Maybe you don't need to lose any weight at all? You might be very comfortable and committed to your exercise program already.

Different goals affect the way in which you should start an exercise program. What I can tell you is to be cautious of canned workout programs that are good "for everybody." At http://tomfabbri.com you'll find examples of routines and exercises I recommend for a variety of fitness goal types. My personal goal at the moment is to climb Mt. McKinley. My workout is designed accordingly to help me do that. But I wouldn't recommend my workout as a wellness maintenance program for everyone.

So for now, just do an honest assessment of where you are and what your goal is. If you did the goal setting work in Chapter One, you have already done that honest assessment. If not, here is your second chance. Take a good look at yourself in the mirror an answer these questions: What do you like about your body, and what would you like to change? When would you like to make those changes? Why?

Life is an Adventure — Live Yours Now

Fun Matters and You Should Have Some

H AVE you ever noticed how willing children are to be happy? It's just one of those things we expect from them. So when you see a four-year old, running down the aisles of a supermarket and giggling out loud, you smile and think it is adorable. If you ever saw a forty-year old man do it you'd climb in with the frozen pizzas and call the police.

When we were young, real joy and happiness were encouraged. Fun and play was just part of childhood and for most of us it was nurtured. Happiness, of the laughing and giggling variety was encouraged.

But for most of us the lessons changed as we got older. We started to hear things like "It's time to get serious," or "Stop messing around," or the real bummer "Quit acting like a kid!" So many of us have learned to believe that real bliss, joy, adventure, and playtime are not a necessary part of adult life. Sure, we haven't given up on fun and adventure altogether, but we have made it one of our goals instead of an everyday (or at least every week) occurrence.

Why did we buy that? What is so wrong with acting like a kid sometimes? That sense of wonder that children have, of adventure, of play, that happiness that they long for and grab at every chance they get, that is the truly divine part of being alive. That we have somehow come to believe that shutting that down is a requirement of adult life is one of the great tragedies in our culture. And it isn't true. Joy and adventure and fun are the best part of being an adult in the first place. What else is your health for but to share with other people and to connect with the world around you? Isn't "to have more fun" one of the best reasons to make the changes we've talked about with nutrition and exercise and attitude?

The funny thing about happiness (yes, that pun was intended) is that they feed off, and are required of each other. The research on laughter and fun and is clear: Laughter is good for you. Or actually, stress is bad for you, while laughter and joy and playtime are powerful stress reducers.

Laughter releases endorphins, which reduces stress and stress hormones. It lowers cortisol levels, creates a sense of well-being, and brings about peace and calm. In terms of staying well and living longer, staying calm and free from the effects of bad stress is vital.

So, just as we need to seek out the right foods to eat, schedule time for our health and take time to meditate and contemplate our goals, we must also take time for fun. We have to build some adventure into our lives.

I'm not talking about climbing Everest.

I mean if climbing mountains is your thing, then I guess I am talking about Everest, but your adventure and fun does not have to be made up of mythic quests and challenges. It does, like everything else you are doing for your health, have to be a regular part of your life now. Adventure and fun and, for God's sake, *real* laughter should be something you do on purpose and often. Taking time off for things that aren't work is essential to your health, makes you even more productive, and is the best part of the ageless lifestyle.

Discover (Again) Your Happiness

If you can't remember the last time you had real fun, it can be difficult to remember what fun actually is to you. I've seen it—it's scary. So if that's you, first spend some time reconnecting with your happiness. With nothing else on your mind, think about what makes you happy (or what used to make you happy) and write it down. Try to come up with at least five things that make you feel happier when you do them. I'm not going to offer suggestions. This one is on you. You may have forgotten, but if you think about it, you will remember who you are and what makes you happy. Try to remember five things and write them down.

Pause your reading and do it now.

Now that you have them written down (and this is the real genius part), do them. I know it sounds so obvious as to be stupid advice, but don't look at me. You're the one who hasn't done that thing you used to like so much. Seriously, right now have a look at your schedule for the next available open time slot that will allow you to do one of your five things and put it on the schedule. (Put the book down and do this....I'll wait.)

Schedule Mini-Adventures

There is absolutely no need to wait until you have a long weekend or even some vacation time available to take a mini-vacation for a quick recharge. Consider scheduling into your week simple three-hour mini-adventures. You can take your kids (or use that time to get away from them), you can go with your significant other (or not), or even schedule some time with friends that you haven't connected with in a while. It doesn't matter. It is only important that you do it. Put it on the schedule. "Thursday—6-9 PM, Meet friends for coffee," or "Wednesday—after work till whenever, walk City Park." Try once a week to schedule in a mini-adventure, away from the home and office, for a quick recharge and time doing something else, anything else, anywhere. It doesn't have to be Paris.

If you don't like the park or coffee, do something else. Get a massage, weekly. Go to the library to read and meditate, weekly. Spend some time doing the activities we discussed in Chapter 2, and make sure you do it weekly. Making these activities part of your schedule makes them real. They deserve the same importance given to any other event on your calendar. You might decide that Tuesday night is movie night, so no matter what, every Tuesday you are going to see a movie (Note: Horror movies are proven to be stressful, cortisol-increasing events that do not count as down time.)

Have Fun Every Day

Something, anything, should be fun for you every day. In my own life I am very fortunate in that I love cooking. The kitchen in my home is where I spend most of my day. There is something about the preparation of food, the chopping of vegetables, preparing things, and the wonderful smells that makes cooking in my kitchen fun to me. So every time I eat at home (or at a friend's who lets me cook) I get thirty minutes to an hour of plain old fun before the meal. Now that I think about it, I even enjoy the cleaning up after a meal. (That career as a chef is really starting to make sense about now.)

If cooking is fun for you, then congrats! You're there. If not, it is still important to do something every day that you enjoy doing. Make it a habit. (Eating is a habit for me so, problem solved.) If you like reading, do it every day. If you happen to love working out (and if you don't yet, be patient, it will come), then your workouts count as fun too. A good friend of mine has a pool table in his garage and shoots for thirty minutes every day after work. If what really jazzes you is bird watching, that's great! Now, do it every day.

You don't have to have the same fun every day forever, but pick something daily and have fun with it on purpose. The reason is that if you can develop a habitual down time rhythm to your life, your body and mind will start to know it is coming, and act accordingly. What you are creating is a daily light at the end of the work tunnel. And yes, even if you are so fortunate to have a job that you love to do and it energizes you, it still involves stresses on your brain and body. Having a daily period of something else that is not at all stressful becomes a very calming, steadying comfort to your life.

"A wasted weekend is not a weekend wasted."

~ Anon

Take Time Off—from Everything

The simple idea that "time doing nothing isn't actually doing nothing" isn't new and has never been bad advice. Your brain, —like everything else—needs, or more correctly grows, from down time. You need time in your schedule when you consider absolutely nothing in particular. It is a lie to think that "achievement" is about toil. It is a lie to think that time off is laziness of any kind. Going to the beach or to the woods, spending time in the mountains or a local park, even simply sitting in your back yard doing nothing at all but noticing the world is a rejuvenating act of growth that will make your life and work better when you return.

Henry David Thoreau put it this way and I believe this thought is worth framing and putting on the wall in your office:

> "There were times when I could not afford to sacrifice the bloom of the present moment to any work, whether of the head or hands. I love a broad margin to my life. Sometimes, in a summer morning, having taken my accustomed bath, I sat in my sunny doorway from sunrise till noon, rapt in a revery, amidst the pines and hickories and sumachs, in undisturbed solitude and stillness, while the birds sing around or flitted noiseless through the house, until by the sun falling in at my west window, or the noise of some traveller's wagon on the distant highway, I was reminded of the lapse of time. I grew in those seasons like corn in the night, and they were far better than any work of the hands would have been. They were not time subtracted from my life, but so much over and above my usual allowance."

~ Henry David Thoreau, *Walden*

In short, long hours of doing nothing is not *doing nothing*.

So Have Fun

You can have adventure and fun at Starbucks. You can interact with the world by walking down the street where you live. You can play almost anywhere. The thing is, because we are adults, you have to do it on purpose. Because if we're not careful, we will find ourselves looking back at this time (your life today) with longing for what we should have done more of, and it won't be the work. It will be the play and the connection and the real time with those we love.

Remember those goals you wrote down? Remember the purpose behind each one? I'm not sure if you noticed or not, but they all had to do with happiness, didn't they? The reason (the why) for every goal you have in life comes down to happiness and to connection. They are all about fun, and love and the adventure of your life. You want more time with those you admire, more time laughing with your friends, and more time loving the person you are. Those are the only worthwhile reasons to be ageless.

You can reach those goals. You have everything you need to make the changes necessary to be healthier and happier. You can feel good about yourself every day. You can be more effective, have more energy, more vitality; you can forget your age and quite literally be ageless. Keep working, keep learning, and believe and start all of that right now. Begin again living the way you deserve and in no time at all, someone will ask you, "How old are you?"

"I'm not," will be the truest answer you can give.

Now go ahead. Run down the aisles and laugh. Tell anyone that looks at you funny to lighten up—that's exactly what you did.

For links to information on stress and its effects on your body, visit www.tomfabbri.com/relax.

10 Ageless Recipes

1. Irish Porridge with Fresh Berries and Agave Syrup

- 1cup steel cut oats
- 1 cup fresh or frozen berries-blueberries, black raspberries or strawberries
- 1 tbsp per serving of Agave syrup
- 1 tbsp per serving of flax seed

IN a medium saucepan combine oats and enough water to cover, bring to a simmer over medium heat, turn off, let cool and place in refrigerator. When ready to use reheat on low stirring occasionally until oats tender and creamy, add water if necessary, cook about 15 minutes.

Spoon porridge into bowls and top with fresh berries, Agave syrup and ground flax seed. Serve at once with 2 medium soft-boiled eggs which will give you about 15 grams of the best protein you can get. By the way the yolk contains half of the protein from the egg and with all the minerals and vitamins.

2. Breakfast Smoothie- Berry Berry Smoothie

With their reputation as a healthful ingredient spreading around the world, Wild Blueberries are turning up everywhere, in products of all kinds. From cereals and muffin mixes to jams and jellies, from teas and juices to yogurt and smoothies, Wild Blueberry is an ingredient that adds taste, color and extra-healthy appeal. The high antioxidant and anti-inflammatory potential of Wild Blueberries make them an ideal ingredient for health drinks and other health-oriented food products. Whether it's improving eyesight, defending against heart disease, cancer and Alzheimer's disease, or  maintaining urinary tract health, Wild Blueberries have what it takes in today's fast-growing functional food marketplace.

- ½ cup fresh or frozen blueberries
- ½ cup fresh or frozen black raspberries
- ½ cup fresh or frozen strawberries
- 1 banana
- 1-cup kefir or plain non-fat yogurt
- 1 scoop whey vanilla protein powder
- 1 tbsp ground flaxseed
- 1 cup crushed ice
- 1-cup ice water

In a blender or food processor combine ingredients until mixture is smooth. 30 to 45 seconds. Pour smoothie into 2 tall glasses and serve at once.

This smoothie is a great source of anti-oxidants and live cultures.

---

3. Multi-Grain Crepes W/Fresh Fruit Compote

Crepes

- 1-cup multi-grain flour
- 2 whole eggs
- 1 tbsp olive oil
- ½ cup kefir

In a large mixing bowl whisk together flour and eggs, add in kefir and oil, beat until smooth. Heat griddle or non-stick pan over medium high heat. Use ¼ cup for each crepe—pour over griddle. Tilt pan in a circular motion so batter coats pan, cook 2 minutes, then flip—use spatula to turn.

Fruit Compote

- ½ cup blueberries
- ½ cup black raspberries
- ½ cup chopped strawberries
- ½ cup red raspberries
- ½ tsp ground ginger
- ¼ tsp ground Cinnamon
- 1 tsp pure vanilla extract
- 1 tbsp lemon juice
- ¼ cup water

Simmer water, lemon juice, and vanilla extract, cinnamon, ginger over low heat, add fruit and simmer until fruit and liquid are slightly thick, serve warm or chilled over crepes.

4. Spicy Cajun Turkey Meatloaf with Cool Tomato Salsa

Comfort food never tasted so good, this rustic dish combined with grilled asparagus and my healthy skillet cornbread will rival any Cajun Chef's from New Orleans.

- 1½ pounds ground turkey breast 93/7%
- 1 large white onion, chopped
- ½ cup panko bread crumbs
- ½ cup chopped fresh parsley
- 2 tbsp Cajun seasoning
- 3 large garlic cloves minced
- 2 large eggs (beaten)
- 2 tsp ground cumin
- 1 tsp dried thyme
- Creole mustard
- 1 jalapeño seeded and minced

In a medium bowl combine all ingredients, chill for one hour in the refrigerator before serving.

Preheat oven, 350 F. Sauté onion and garlic in sauté pan coated with non stick spray, cook until clear, careful not to burn garlic. Remove from pan to bowl, set aside to cool.

Combine turkey, breadcrumb, parsley, Cajun seasoning, eggs, cumin, and thyme and jalapeno and onion/garlic mixture when cooled. Place mixture in a 9x5- nonstick loaf pan. Cover with foil and bake for 20 minutes. Take out of oven; spread Creole mustard on top, place back in oven uncovered for another 35 minutes. Use a meat thermometer to take the guesswork out of cooking ground turkey to assure that a safe temperature has been reached to destroy any harmful bacteria. For ground turkey, that temp is 165 F.
Remove from oven and let stand for 10 minutes.

Cool Tomato Salsa

- 3 tomatoes seeded and chopped
- ½ cup finely minced white onion
- 5 Serrano Chiles finely minced
- ½ cup fresh cilantro chopped
- 1 teaspoon sea salt
- *2 teaspoons lime juice* Remove from pan and cut into slices and top with cool tomato salsa.

5. Not Your Mother's Chicken Noodle Soup

If there is a way to fight the common cold, this is it. Full of flavor, texture, fiber, protein and aromatic ingredients such as ginger, garlic and fresh cilantro, this hearty dish is the ultimate comfort food when you are under the weather or maintaining that sense of well being, physically and emotionally.

- ½ cup brown rice
- ½ cup wild rice
- 1 yellow onion chopped
- 2 tbsp fresh ginger minced
- 2 cloves garlic minced
- 1 carrot peeled and diced
- 1 celery stalk chopped
- ½ cup green onion thinly sliced
- ½ cup fresh cilantro chopped
- 2 tbsp coconut oil
- 5 cups fat free, low sodium chicken broth
- 3 chicken breast, bone in, skin removed
- 2 chicken thighs, bone in, skin removed
- Pinch of sea salt and cracked pepper

In a saucepan add 2 cups of water and bring to a boil. Add the wild and brown rice, reduce the heat and bring to a simmer. Cover and cook rice for about 45 to 50 minutes or until rice in tender. Drain water, set rice aside.

In a large saucepan heat coconut oil over medium heat, add the onion and sauté until soft and clear, about 5 to 7 minutes. Add the garlic and ginger and continue to sauté. After about 2 minutes add the chicken broth, carrot, chicken, wild and brown rice and 2 more cups of water, bring to a simmer. Reduce heat and cover. Cook for about 15 to 20 minutes and chicken is thoroughly cooked.

Transfer chicken pieces to a cutting board and let cool. Remove the bones and shred the chicken into bite size portions. Add chicken back into saucepan along with cilantro and green onion. Season to taste with sea salt and freshly cracked pepper. Serve at once.

Makes 8 servings—good source of protein and antioxidants

6. Summer Berries with Manchego Cheese

With blueberries being the leader in antioxidants, along with blackberries, raspberries and strawberries, this dessert packs a punch when it comes to strengthening the immune system. Take a stroll through the farmer's market and pick up some of these super foods. Not only are they sweet and delicious but they add vitamins and minerals to your menu.

- 1 cup fresh blueberries
- 1 cup fresh blackberries
- 1 cup raspberries
- 1 cup strawberries diced
- 4 sprigs fresh mint
- ¼ cup powdered sugar
- 1 cup Port wine
- 4 oz manchego cheese sliced thin

Place berries in a colander and rinse thoroughly. Then place berries in a large bowl and pour Port wine over the berries, place in refrigerator for at least 2 hours.

To plate, place 2 slices of cheese on a small dessert plate as depicted, spoon berries, about 1 cup onto cheese, then top with ½ slice of cheese and a sprig of mint, sprinkle with powdered sugar. Serve at once.

4 servings—great source of antioxidants and calcium.

7. Fresh Guacamole with a Squeeze of Orange Juice

- 2 Avocado's peeled and pit removed
- ½ onion minced
- ½ jalapeno seeds removed, minced
- 1 tomato flesh removed chopped
- 1 bunch cilantro chopped
- 1 clove garlic minced
- Squeeze from ½ lemon
- Squeeze from ½ orange
- Sea Salt pinch to taste

Combine all ingredients in a mixing bowl, mash with a fork to leave Guacamole chunky. Place pits in Guacamole to keep fresh. Spread fresh guacamole on 7-sprouted grain bread for a healthy snack.

I consider a snack a meal, so when I reach for a healthy snack I always reach for a glass of Lemon water. At every meal I am drinking at least 8 ounces of lemon water. Keeping your body hydrated is fundamental for optimum performance and living a long healthy life. Adding lemon to your water will reduce the risk of heart disease, stroke and cancer.

---

8. Fish Tacos with Mesculin Mix and Avocado Crème

This traditional California dish brings a balance of Health and Mexican culture to your table. Simple, light and full of flavor, this ultimate fish taco is a hit at all my outdoor grilling events.

Avocado Crème

- 1 ripe avocado
- 1 cup plain non-fat yogurt
- 2 tbsp lime juice
- 2 tsp cumin
- Sea Salt and fresh cracked pepper

Slice avocado in have, remove the pit and scoop out the flesh into a blender or food processor. Add yogurt, lime juice, cumin, and sea salt. Blend until mixture is smooth. Place in a ceramic bowl, cover and chill in refrigerator.

Mesculin and Cabbage Slaw 2 cups Mesculin Mix

- 2 cups Savoy cabbage shredded
- ½ cup English cucumber diced
- ½ cup red bell pepper diced
- 1 Serrano Chile seeded and minced
- 2 tbsp extra-virgin olive oil
- 3 tbsp Cilantro chopped
- 2 tbsp Onion minced

To make the Mesculin and Cabbage mix combine Mesculin greens with shredded cabbage, cucumber, bell pepper, chile, cilantro and onion, olive oil. Mix well.
Chilean Sea Bass, Halibut or other firm fleshed white fish

- 1 lb, skin removed

Prepping the grill, spray rack with non-stick spray, heat grill to high. Coat fish lightly with olive oil, salt and pepper. Grill fish 3 to 4 minutes on each side. Remove and place on platter, cover with foil to keep warm.

Corn Tortillas, 8—2 per serving

Wrap corn tortillas in foil and heat on the grill for about 3 to 5 minutes. To serve, place 2 tortillas on a plate, place salad mixture on each tortilla, top with a portion of fish and drizzle with avocado crème, serve at once.

Makes 4 servings and is a great source of fiber and omega-3's

9. Oven Roasted Chilean Sea Bass over Sautéed Spinach

Chilean Sea Bass is a white fish rich in Omega-3 unsaturated oils and is a great source of lean protein. With a unique large flake like texture, the fish is mild with an unexpected and delicious buttery flavor. Combine this fish with sautéed spinach and you have a very powerful dish.

The premise is that certain foods are nutritional powerhouses, and should be piled into grocery carts and lunch boxes. Blueberries bubble with cancer-fighting, heart-healthy antioxidants, avocados ooze with the same good fats that olive oil has, and spinach, well, spinach has it all, as Popeye always knew.

- 2 6-8oz. Chilean Sea Bass Filets
- 2 Large vine ripened tomatoes, cut into eighths
- 1 red onion cut into eighths
- 2 garlic gloves minced
- ¼ cup parsley chopped
- ½ cup dry white wine
- 3 tablespoons extra virgin olive oil
- Sea salt and freshly ground pepper

- Spinach (ingredients)
- ¾ lb fresh baby Spinach, washed and dried
- 2 tablespoons extra virgin olive oil
- Freshly ground black pepper
- Pinch of red pepper flakes

Preheat oven to 400. Season fillets with salt and pepper. Coat an oven-proof baking dish (I use an iron skillet), with olive oil. Place fish in the baking dish. Break onions apart and mix with tomatoes and garlic, place mixture around the fish, making sure to get them nicely coated with the oil (add an additional tablespoon if you need it). Pour the white wine over the fish and vegetables and sprinkle parsley over the top, you can also add more black pepper if you like.

Cover with foil and let sit for 20-30 minutes.

Remove foil and place fish in oven for 15-20 minutes until fish is opaque and cooked through and tomatoes/onions have softened. Turn off oven and let fish rest for 5 minutes. While fish is resting, heat the olive oil for spinach, in a large sauté pan, over high heat until very hot. Add the spinach and cook, stirring frequently, for about 1 to 2 minutes, the spinach should turn bright green and wilt slightly. Remove the spinach from the heat, add the red pepper and black pepper, toss well. Place spinach on serving dish and top with a sea bass filet, tomatoes and onions. Spoon any remaining sauce in the baking dish over fish and vegetables.

10. Salad in a Glass

- 2 carrots peeled
- ¼ inch slice Ginger Root
- 1 Red Gala Apple cored
- 2 Kale Leaves
- ½ cup parsley

Juice the carrots, apple and ginger, then the kale and parsley. I then take the juice, add ½ cup of ice and blend in my magic bullet to make a delicious chilled Salad in a Glass.

How Juicing Helps Your Bones

Juicing is an easy way to consume high concentrates of all the nutrients, vitamins and minerals necessary for good bone health. Juicing also helps balance the body's acid-alkaline balance. Meats and Dairy products create an acidic environment in the body, where as juicing with fruits and vegetables are high in alkaline ingredients.

Full Advantage Workout

Stretch and Work Your Support System

Warm-Up to Win Big in the Exercise Game

A warm-up must be a part of your exercise regimen. These would consist of exercises performed immediately before your main activity to increase your circulation and your heart rate.

A big misconception is that stretching is warming up. In fact, static stretching does nothing to increase core temperatures and circulation. Any good trainer will tell you that a general warm up should be preceded by a stretching routine. What is a general warm up? It can be light calisthenics, jogging, jumping rope or 5 minutes on a recumbent bike. A warm up session should last for a minimum of 5 minutes and the goal is to increase blood flow and raise your core temperature.

Here are some of the benefits of a warm up:

- Increase blood flow
- Increase core temperature
- Increase heart rate
- Increase muscle efficiency
- Great preparation for the individual psychologically

Being more flexible

When it comes to physical fitness with the everyday at home athlete, stretching and flexibility are a total unknown or all but forgotten. And whether you are a stay at home mom or busy executive, your body is your instrument and proper stretching must be incorporated into your routine if you want to live an Ageless Lifestyle.

By being more flexible you can reduce the rate at which you age and flexibility can be developed at any age. I have incorporated here 10 Flexibility and Stretching exercises which along with exercise, sound nutrition and supplementation are factors, which you will use to your Full Advantage to get to that Ageless You.

10 Basic Static Stretches that Will Stretch Your Life

Static stretching is stretching to the farthest point and holding that stretch. Standing straight and bending over to touch your palms to the floor is a good example of a static stretch, which 9 out of 10 Americans cannot perform.

Static stretching is very similar to Hatha Yoga, which has been around since the 15th century. Static stretching is by far the safest of stretching methods.

Advantages of Static Stretching

- Simplicity
- Easy execution
- Induces muscular relaxation

10 Guidelines

1. Warm up before stretching.
2. Have a positive attitude.
3. Breathe at a normal rate.
4. Develop a smooth tempo.
5. Use proper posture and form.
6. Move slowly into the stretch.

7. Do not force a stretch.
8. Let gravity pull you into a stretch.
9. Hold the stretch between 10 and 30 seconds.
10. Concentrate and focus.

Stretch #1 — Hamstrings/Lower Back/Upper Back/Quads

Position yourself on the floor with one leg straight and the other leg bent at the knee with the heel touching the outside of the opposite thigh.. Move your upper body forward towards your extended leg, hold between 10 and 30 seconds, switch legs and repeat. Breathe through the motion.

Stretch #2—Adductors/Hips/Gluteals

Seated on the floor with both legs extended outward, lower your upper body to the floor resting on your elbows. Hold for 10 to 30 seconds.

Stretch #3—Arms/Shoulders/Neck

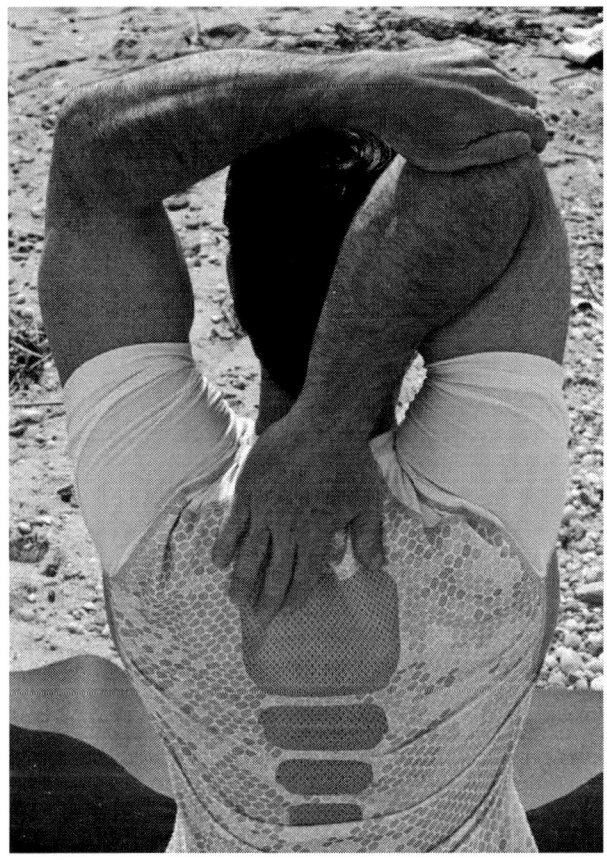

While seated as in Stretch #2, flex one arm raised over your head. Grab your elbow with the opposite hand and pull your elbow behind your head.

Stretch #4—Quads/Shoulders/Lower Back

Kneel on all fours, palms facing downward. Now slide your palms forward until your forehead touches the ground.

Stretch #5—Quadriceps/Chest/Shoulders/Abs

With your knees together, kneel on the floor and sit back on your heels with your toes pointed backwards. Now lean back and place the palms of your hands on the floor behind you pointed away from your body.

Stretch #6—Pectorals

Kneel on the floor, on all fours, and slide your palms forward until your arms are stretched outward. Your forehead should be touching the floor while arching your back downward.

Stretch #7—Adductors/Upper Back/Lower Back/Chest

While kneeling on the floor, elbows and palms also on the floor in front of you, spread your knees and slide your hands forward while touching your chest to the floor.

Stretch #8—Hamstrings/Calves/Lower Back/Upper Back

From a standing position, bend over to place the palms of your hands on the floor. Now walk your hands forward about two feet until you feel the tension in your hamstrings relax while keeping your heels planted on the floor.

Stretch #9—Lower Back/Gluteals/Hamstrings

While lying on your back, bring your knees to your chest, grab behind your knees and pull your legs towards your chest with your knees bent.

Stretch #10—Neck/Trapezius/Shoulders

While seated on the floor, your legs spread wide, your arms by your side, palms flat on the floor so that it matches the picture, move your head from side to side, front to back. Now shrug your shoulders in an up and down motion, then roll your shoulders forward in a circular motion, then backward in a circular motion.

One Final Note about Stretching

If you are serious about your Health and Full Advantage Workouts, and I'm sure you are, spending 10 to 15 minutes stretching a day may be the most important part of your regimen. Along with increased flexibility for an Ageless Lifestyle, it may also decrease injury during workouts.

---

10 Basic Exercises at the Heart of the Full Advantage Workout System

L ISTED here are 10 basic exercises for anyone beginning a new routine, plus some alternate isometric exercises if gym equipment is not available. While this is not a complete list of every exercise imaginable for every body part, the ones listed represent the core of all movements in the Full Advantage Workout System.

1. Flat Body Bar Bench Press (Works Mid-Chest)

Wide grip on the body bar.
Feet planted firmly on the floor.
Keep your core tight.
Arms flexed. Chest flexed.

Lower the bar to mid chest.

Keep everything flexed during the movement. Flex the back and shoulders while stretching the chest.

The **advantage** of my *Full Advantage Workout System* is that while keeping the other secondary muscles flexed, you get a complete workout on the chest and back, plus triceps, biceps and shoulders.

The Key: Remain focused on the intensity throughout the entire movement.

Isometric Version of the Chest Exercise

Illustration #1

With arms straight ahead and palms together (see illustation #1) and keeping everything flexed in chest, arms, core, and legs, bring your hands towards your body, stretching the chest and flexing the back and shoulders (see illustration #2).

The Full Advantage Workout applies to isometrics as well.

Illustration #2

2. Back

Shoulder width grip on the body bar.

Feet planted firmly on the floor. Keep your core tight.

Your body is upright but slightly bent forward at the waist. All your muscles are flexed, chest, back, shoulders, legs.

Raise the bar to your chest, flexing your back while stretching your chest.

Keep everything flexed during the movement.

Isometric Version of the Back Exercise

Illustration #1

With your body upright but slightly bent forward at the waist (see illustration #1), keeping everything flexed, including chest, arms, core, and legs, bring your hands towards your body, stretching the chest and flexing the back and shoulders (see illustration #2).

The Full Advantage Workout applies to isometrics as well.

Illustration #2

3. Standing Body Bar Shoulder Press

Shoulder width grip on the body bar.
Feet planted firmly on the floor.
Keep your core tight.

All your muscles are flexed, chest, back, shoulders, legs.

Extend the Body Bar overhead. Flex the shoulders. Do not lock out the arms.

Isometric Version of the Standing Shoulder Press

Gripping a towel, hands shoulder width apart and arms overhead, pull outward creating tension on the towel.

Now pull downward until the towel is shoulder level, flexing the back muscles but always keeping that outward tension on the towel. Now press upward using your shoulders until elbows are straight.

4. Standing Body Bar Biceps Curl

Shoulder width grip on the body bar.
Feet planted firmly on the floor.

Keep your core tight. All your muscles are flexed, chest, back, shoulders, legs.

From the lower position, body bar next to your thighs, slowly curl the bar upwards always maintaining that focused intensity on the bicep muscles being worked, as well as the other muscles being flexed.

Now lower the bar in the same manner down to your thighs always remaining in the flexed position.

Isometric Version of Biceps and Triceps

Grip a towel, hands close together, one palm up and one palm down.

With the palm facing up, hand curl the arm towards your body while with the hand facing down, arm press away from your body. So flex the bicep, then the triceps. Now switch sides.

5. Triceps

Lie on your back on the floor, or a bench. Shoulder width grip on the body bar. Feet planted firmly on the floor. Keep your core tight. Arms flexed. Chest flexed.

Lower the bar bending at the elbows to your forehead. Keep everything flexed during the movement, shoulders, triceps, biceps, back, core and chest. Slowly straighten arms to starting position, still keeping everything flexed.

6. Body Bar Lunges

Stand with feet shoulder width apart. Place Body Bar behind neck.

Shoulder width grip on the body bar. Knees slightly bent, chest out, shoulders back. Keep your core tight. Arms flexed. Chest flexed.

Lunge foreword while stretching hamstrings and gluteus. Keep everything flexed during the movement.

Return to starting position, lunge with opposite leg.

Lunges without Body Bar

Performed essentially the same way as with the body bar, except place the hands on the hips.

7. Hamstrings and Gluteals

Lying on the floor in a Yoga position, called Up-ward facing Dog: Chest out, shoulders back. Keep your core tight. Arms flexed. Keep legs and gluts flexed.

Slowly curl legs towards buttocks. Keep everything flexed during the movement. Return to starting position.

8. Calves

The heel is raised and lowered while standing on a raised block. The balls of the feet are planted firmly on a raised block.

Keep your core tight. Arms flexed. Chest flexed. The heel is raised as high as possible flexing the calf muscle.

The heel is lowered stretching the calf muscle.

9. Forearms

Holding the bar behind you as illustrated. Keep your core tight, arms flexed, Chest out and Shoulders back and flexed.

The wrist is bent away from the body so that the palm moves toward the flexed forearms. The motion is to curl and then straighten the wrists.

The heel is raised as high as possible flexing the calf muscle.

The heel is lowered stretching the calf muscle.

10. Abdominals

Lie on your back, legs bent with your feet on the floor. Position body bar across the upper chest holding it with your arms crossed. This exercise can be done without the body bar as well. Keep your core tight. Arms flexed. Chest out and shoulders back and flexed.

Bend forward slowly raising your upper body off the floor. Hold for 1 second.

Return to starting position.

Conclusion

I have always had this driving passion to be living the life of my dreams——doing what I love to do, becoming the best, and showing others that they can do exactly the same. My belief is that being successful in any area of life begins with peak health and fitness.

Ageless You is the foundation to that destination. It is about that second chance for anyone who wants to have that do-over or new beginning. This book shows you the essentials of reaching your true physical, mental and spiritual self.

My goal is to help you achieve your goals. Use this book to motivate, educate and empower yourself to reach your dreams, to be strong, calm, and confident as you become and live that ageless you.

One last thing... as you and I venture down this path of agelessness together, promise me that you will contact me www.tomfabbri.com and share your experiences of what has changed in your life.

Thank you.
Tom Fabbri